Music

Celtic Classics
for String Trio
(with optional Violin 2 for Viola)

Arranged by Carole N. Rabinowitz

Instrumentation

1 Full Score
1 Violin 1
1 Violin 2
(for Viola)
1 Viola
1 Cello

1. Dance to Your Shadow
2. My Love is Like a Red, Red Rose
3. Flow Gently, Sweet Afton
4. Morgan Magan
5. Highland Cathedral
6. Lily of the West
7. Mick McGuire

GRADE 3
52702360

Latham
Music

A Division of **LudwigMasters** Publications
6403 West Rogers Circle • Boca Raton, FL 33487

Celtic Classics
for String Trio
1. Dance to Your Shadow

Folksong from the Hebrides
Arranged by Carole N. Rabinowitz

2. My Love is Like a Red, Red Rose

Scottish Folk Song
Arranged by Carole N. Rabinowitz

3. Flow Gently, Sweet Afton

Scottish Folk Song
Arranged by Carole N. Rabinowitz

6

4. Morgan Magan

Irish Folk Song
Arranged by Carole N. Rabinowitz

(Viola lower octave)

(no rit.)

D.C. al Fine

5. Highland Cathedral

Traditional Scottish
Arranged by Carole N. Rabinowitz

(Viola lower octave)

6. Lily of the West

Traditional
Arranged by Carole N. Rabinowitz

13

52702361

7. Mick McGuire

Irish Folksong
Arranged by Carole N. Rabinowitz

16

A Division of **LudwigMasters Publications**
6403 West Rogers Circle • Boca Raton, Florida 33487
(800) 434-6340 • (561) 241-6169
Fax: (561) 241-6347 • www.ludwigmasters.com